This book belongs to:

_____

A

Name

Address

Home   Mobile

Work   Email

Anniversary   Birthday

Notes

Name

Address

Home   Mobile

Work   Email

Anniversary   Birthday

Notes

Name

Address

Home   Mobile

Work   Email

Anniversary   Birthday

Notes

A

Name

Address

Home   Mobile

Work   Email

Anniversary   Birthday

Notes

Name

Address

Home   Mobile

Work   Email

Anniversary   Birthday

Notes

Name

Address

Home   Mobile

Work   Email

Anniversary   Birthday

Notes

A

Name

Address

Home   Mobile

Work   Email

Anniversary   Birthday

Notes

Name

Address

Home   Mobile

Work   Email

Anniversary   Birthday

Notes

Name

Address

Home   Mobile

Work   Email

Anniversary   Birthday

Notes

A

Name

Address

Home   Mobile

Work   Email

Anniversary   Birthday

Notes

Name

Address

Home   Mobile

Work   Email

Anniversary   Birthday

Notes

Name

Address

Home   Mobile

Work   Email

Anniversary   Birthday

Notes

A

Name

Address

Home   Mobile

Work   Email

Anniversary   Birthday

Notes

Name

Address

Home   Mobile

Work   Email

Anniversary   Birthday

Notes

Name

Address

Home   Mobile

Work   Email

Anniversary   Birthday

Notes

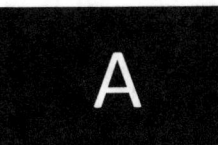

A

Name

Address

Home   Mobile

Work   Email

Anniversary   Birthday

Notes

Name

Address

Home   Mobile

Work   Email

Anniversary   Birthday

Notes

Name

Address

Home   Mobile

Work   Email

Anniversary   Birthday

Notes

B

Name

Address

Home	Mobile
Work	Email
Anniversary	Birthday

Notes

Name

Address

Home	Mobile
Work	Email
Anniversary	Birthday

Notes

Name

Address

Home	Mobile
Work	Email
Anniversary	Birthday

Notes

B

Name

Address

Home   Mobile

Work   Email

Anniversary   Birthday

Notes

Name

Address

Home   Mobile

Work   Email

Anniversary   Birthday

Notes

Name

Address

Home   Mobile

Work   Email

Anniversary   Birthday

Notes

B

Name

Address

Home   Mobile

Work   Email

Anniversary   Birthday

Notes

Name

Address

Home   Mobile

Work   Email

Anniversary   Birthday

Notes

Name

Address

Home   Mobile

Work   Email

Anniversary   Birthday

Notes

B

Name

Address

Home | Mobile

Work | Email

Anniversary | Birthday

Notes

Name

Address

Home | Mobile

Work | Email

Anniversary | Birthday

Notes

Name

Address

Home | Mobile

Work | Email

Anniversary | Birthday

Notes

B

Name

Address

Home | Mobile
Work | Email
Anniversary | Birthday
Notes

Name

Address

Home | Mobile
Work | Email
Anniversary | Birthday
Notes

Name

Address

Home | Mobile
Work | Email
Anniversary | Birthday
Notes

B

Name

Address

Home   Mobile

Work   Email

Anniversary   Birthday

Notes

Name

Address

Home   Mobile

Work   Email

Anniversary   Birthday

Notes

Name

Address

Home   Mobile

Work   Email

Anniversary   Birthday

Notes

C

Name

Address

Home | Mobile

Work | Email

Anniversary | Birthday

Notes

Name

Address

Home | Mobile

Work | Email

Anniversary | Birthday

Notes

Name

Address

Home | Mobile

Work | Email

Anniversary | Birthday

Notes

C

Name

Address

Home   Mobile

Work   Email

Anniversary   Birthday

Notes

Name

Address

Home   Mobile

Work   Email

Anniversary   Birthday

Notes

Name

Address

Home   Mobile

Work   Email

Anniversary   Birthday

Notes

C

Name

Address

Home   Mobile

Work   Email

Anniversary   Birthday

Notes

Name

Address

Home   Mobile

Work   Email

Anniversary   Birthday

Notes

Name

Address

Home   Mobile

Work   Email

Anniversary   Birthday

Notes

C

Name

Address

Home   Mobile

Work   Email

Anniversary   Birthday

Notes

Name

Address

Home   Mobile

Work   Email

Anniversary   Birthday

Notes

Name

Address

Home   Mobile

Work   Email

Anniversary   Birthday

Notes

C

Name

Address

Home   Mobile

Work   Email

Anniversary   Birthday

Notes

Name

Address

Home   Mobile

Work   Email

Anniversary   Birthday

Notes

Name

Address

Home   Mobile

Work   Email

Anniversary   Birthday

Notes

C

Name

Address

Home   Mobile

Work   Email

Anniversary   Birthday

Notes

Name

Address

Home   Mobile

Work   Email

Anniversary   Birthday

Notes

Name

Address

Home   Mobile

Work   Email

Anniversary   Birthday

Notes

D

Name

Address

Home   Mobile

Work   Email

Anniversary   Birthday

Notes

Name

Address

Home   Mobile

Work   Email

Anniversary   Birthday

Notes

Name

Address

Home   Mobile

Work   Email

Anniversary   Birthday

Notes

D

Name

Address

Home   Mobile

Work   Email

Anniversary   Birthday

Notes

Name

Address

Home   Mobile

Work   Email

Anniversary   Birthday

Notes

Name

Address

Home   Mobile

Work   Email

Anniversary   Birthday

Notes

D

Name

Address

Home   Mobile

Work   Email

Anniversary   Birthday

Notes

Name

Address

Home   Mobile

Work   Email

Anniversary   Birthday

Notes

Name

Address

Home   Mobile

Work   Email

Anniversary   Birthday

Notes

D

Name

Address

Home   **Mobile**

Work   **Email**

Anniversary   **Birthday**

Notes

Name

Address

Home   **Mobile**

Work   **Email**

Anniversary   **Birthday**

Notes

Name

Address

Home   **Mobile**

Work   **Email**

Anniversary   **Birthday**

Notes

D

Name

Address

Home   Mobile

Work   Email

Anniversary   Birthday

Notes

Name

Address

Home   Mobile

Work   Email

Anniversary   Birthday

Notes

Name

Address

Home   Mobile

Work   Email

Anniversary   Birthday

Notes

D

Name

Address

Home   Mobile

Work   Email

Anniversary   Birthday

Notes

Name

Address

Home   Mobile

Work   Email

Anniversary   Birthday

Notes

Name

Address

Home   Mobile

Work   Email

Anniversary   Birthday

Notes

E

Name

Address

Home | Mobile

Work | Email

Anniversary | Birthday

Notes

Name

Address

Home | Mobile

Work | Email

Anniversary | Birthday

Notes

Name

Address

Home | Mobile

Work | Email

Anniversary | Birthday

Notes

Name

Address

Home   Mobile

Work   Email

Anniversary   Birthday

Notes

Name

Address

Home   Mobile

Work   Email

Anniversary   Birthday

Notes

Name

Address

Home   Mobile

Work   Email

Anniversary   Birthday

Notes

E

Name

Address

Home   Mobile

Work   Email

Anniversary   Birthday

Notes

Name

Address

Home   Mobile

Work   Email

Anniversary   Birthday

Notes

Name

Address

Home   Mobile

Work   Email

Anniversary   Birthday

Notes

E

Name

Address

Home   **Mobile**

Work   **Email**

Anniversary   **Birthday**

Notes

Name

Address

Home   **Mobile**

Work   **Email**

Anniversary   **Birthday**

Notes

Name

Address

Home   **Mobile**

Work   **Email**

Anniversary   **Birthday**

Notes

E

Name

Address

Home   Mobile

Work   Email

Anniversary   Birthday

Notes

Name

Address

Home   Mobile

Work   Email

Anniversary   Birthday

Notes

Name

Address

Home   Mobile

Work   Email

Anniversary   Birthday

Notes

E

Name

Address

Home   Mobile

Work   Email

Anniversary   Birthday

Notes

Name

Address

Home   Mobile

Work   Email

Anniversary   Birthday

Notes

Name

Address

Home   Mobile

Work   Email

Anniversary   Birthday

Notes

F

Name

Address

Home   Mobile

Work   Email

Anniversary   Birthday

Notes

Name

Address

Home   Mobile

Work   Email

Anniversary   Birthday

Notes

Name

Address

Home   Mobile

Work   Email

Anniversary   Birthday

Notes

F

Name

Address

Home   **Mobile**

Work   **Email**

Anniversary   **Birthday**

Notes

Name

Address

Home   **Mobile**

Work   **Email**

Anniversary   **Birthday**

Notes

Name

Address

Home   **Mobile**

Work   **Email**

Anniversary   **Birthday**

Notes

F

Name

Address

Home   Mobile

Work   Email

Anniversary   Birthday

Notes

Name

Address

Home   Mobile

Work   Email

Anniversary   Birthday

Notes

Name

Address

Home   Mobile

Work   Email

Anniversary   Birthday

Notes

F

Name

Address

Home   Mobile

Work   Email

Anniversary   Birthday

Notes

Name

Address

Home   Mobile

Work   Email

Anniversary   Birthday

Notes

Name

Address

Home   Mobile

Work   Email

Anniversary   Birthday

Notes

F

Name

Address

Home   Mobile

Work   Email

Anniversary   Birthday

Notes

Name

Address

Home   Mobile

Work   Email

Anniversary   Birthday

Notes

Name

Address

Home   Mobile

Work   Email

Anniversary   Birthday

Notes

F

Name

Address

Home   **Mobile**

Work   **Email**

Anniversary   **Birthday**

Notes

Name

Address

Home   **Mobile**

Work   **Email**

Anniversary   **Birthday**

Notes

Name

Address

Home   **Mobile**

Work   **Email**

Anniversary   **Birthday**

Notes

G

Name

Address

Home   Mobile

Work   Email

Anniversary   Birthday

Notes

Name

Address

Home   Mobile

Work   Email

Anniversary   Birthday

Notes

Name

Address

Home   Mobile

Work   Email

Anniversary   Birthday

Notes

G

Name

Address

Home   **Mobile**

Work   **Email**

Anniversary   **Birthday**

Notes

Name

Address

Home   **Mobile**

Work   **Email**

Anniversary   **Birthday**

Notes

Name

Address

Home   **Mobile**

Work   **Email**

Anniversary   **Birthday**

Notes

G

Name

Address

Home   Mobile

Work   Email

Anniversary   Birthday

Notes

Name

Address

Home   Mobile

Work   Email

Anniversary   Birthday

Notes

Name

Address

Home   Mobile

Work   Email

Anniversary   Birthday

Notes

G

Name

Address

Home

Mobile

Work

Email

Anniversary

Birthday

Notes

Name

Address

Home

Mobile

Work

Email

Anniversary

Birthday

Notes

Name

Address

Home

Mobile

Work

Email

Anniversary

Birthday

Notes

G

Name

Address

Home   Mobile

Work   Email

Anniversary   Birthday

Notes

Name

Address

Home   Mobile

Work   Email

Anniversary   Birthday

Notes

Name

Address

Home   Mobile

Work   Email

Anniversary   Birthday

Notes

G

Name

Address

Home   Mobile

Work   Email

Anniversary   Birthday

Notes

Name

Address

Home   Mobile

Work   Email

Anniversary   Birthday

Notes

Name

Address

Home   Mobile

Work   Email

Anniversary   Birthday

Notes

H

Name

Address

Home   Mobile

Work   Email

Anniversary   Birthday

Notes

Name

Address

Home   Mobile

Work   Email

Anniversary   Birthday

Notes

Name

Address

Home   Mobile

Work   Email

Anniversary   Birthday

Notes

Name

Address

Home	Mobile
Work	Email
Anniversary	Birthday

Notes

Name

Address

Home	Mobile
Work	Email
Anniversary	Birthday

Notes

Name

Address

Home	Mobile
Work	Email
Anniversary	Birthday

Notes

H

Name

Address

Home   Mobile

Work   Email

Anniversary   Birthday

Notes

Name

Address

Home   Mobile

Work   Email

Anniversary   Birthday

Notes

Name

Address

Home   Mobile

Work   Email

Anniversary   Birthday

Notes

H

Name

Address

Home   Mobile

Work   Email

Anniversary   Birthday

Notes

Name

Address

Home   Mobile

Work   Email

Anniversary   Birthday

Notes

Name

Address

Home   Mobile

Work   Email

Anniversary   Birthday

Notes

Name

Address

Home   Mobile

Work   Email

Anniversary   Birthday

Notes

Name

Address

Home   Mobile

Work   Email

Anniversary   Birthday

Notes

Name

Address

Home   Mobile

Work   Email

Anniversary   Birthday

Notes

H

Name

Address

Home   Mobile

Work   Email

Anniversary   Birthday

Notes

Name

Address

Home   Mobile

Work   Email

Anniversary   Birthday

Notes

Name

Address

Home   Mobile

Work   Email

Anniversary   Birthday

Notes

I

Name

Address

Home   Mobile

Work   Email

Anniversary   Birthday

Notes

Name

Address

Home   Mobile

Work   Email

Anniversary   Birthday

Notes

Name

Address

Home   Mobile

Work   Email

Anniversary   Birthday

Notes

I

Name

Address

Home | Mobile

Work | Email

Anniversary | Birthday

Notes

Name

Address

Home | Mobile

Work | Email

Anniversary | Birthday

Notes

Name

Address

Home | Mobile

Work | Email

Anniversary | Birthday

Notes

I

Name

Address

Home   Mobile

Work   Email

Anniversary   Birthday

Notes

Name

Address

Home   Mobile

Work   Email

Anniversary   Birthday

Notes

Name

Address

Home   Mobile

Work   Email

Anniversary   Birthday

Notes

Name

Address

Home   Mobile

Work   Email

Anniversary   Birthday

Notes

Name

Address

Home   Mobile

Work   Email

Anniversary   Birthday

Notes

Name

Address

Home   Mobile

Work   Email

Anniversary   Birthday

Notes

I

Name

Address

Home   Mobile

Work   Email

Anniversary   Birthday

Notes

Name

Address

Home   Mobile

Work   Email

Anniversary   Birthday

Notes

Name

Address

Home   Mobile

Work   Email

Anniversary   Birthday

Notes

I

Name

Address

Home	Mobile
Work	Email
Anniversary	Birthday

Notes

Name

Address

Home	Mobile
Work	Email
Anniversary	Birthday

Notes

Name

Address

Home	Mobile
Work	Email
Anniversary	Birthday

Notes

J

Name

Address

Home   Mobile

Work   Email

Anniversary   Birthday

Notes

Name

Address

Home   Mobile

Work   Email

Anniversary   Birthday

Notes

Name

Address

Home   Mobile

Work   Email

Anniversary   Birthday

Notes

J

Name

Address

Home   Mobile

Work   Email

Anniversary   Birthday

Notes

Name

Address

Home   Mobile

Work   Email

Anniversary   Birthday

Notes

Name

Address

Home   Mobile

Work   Email

Anniversary   Birthday

Notes

J

Name

Address

Home   Mobile

Work   Email

Anniversary   Birthday

Notes

Name

Address

Home   Mobile

Work   Email

Anniversary   Birthday

Notes

Name

Address

Home   Mobile

Work   Email

Anniversary   Birthday

Notes

J

Name

Address

Home   Mobile

Work   Email

Anniversary   Birthday

Notes

Name

Address

Home   Mobile

Work   Email

Anniversary   Birthday

Notes

Name

Address

Home   Mobile

Work   Email

Anniversary   Birthday

Notes

J

Name

Address

Home   Mobile

Work   Email

Anniversary   Birthday

Notes

Name

Address

Home   Mobile

Work   Email

Anniversary   Birthday

Notes

Name

Address

Home   Mobile

Work   Email

Anniversary   Birthday

Notes

J

Name

Address

Home	Mobile
Work	Email
Anniversary	Birthday

Notes

Name

Address

Home	Mobile
Work	Email
Anniversary	Birthday

Notes

Name

Address

Home	Mobile
Work	Email
Anniversary	Birthday

Notes

K

Name

Address

Home   Mobile

Work   Email

Anniversary   Birthday

Notes

Name

Address

Home   Mobile

Work   Email

Anniversary   Birthday

Notes

Name

Address

Home   Mobile

Work   Email

Anniversary   Birthday

Notes

Name

Address

Home   Mobile

Work   Email

Anniversary   Birthday

Notes

Name

Address

Home   Mobile

Work   Email

Anniversary   Birthday

Notes

Name

Address

Home   Mobile

Work   Email

Anniversary   Birthday

Notes

K

Name

Address

Home   Mobile

Work   Email

Anniversary   Birthday

Notes

Name

Address

Home   Mobile

Work   Email

Anniversary   Birthday

Notes

Name

Address

Home   Mobile

Work   Email

Anniversary   Birthday

Notes

Name

Address

Home   Mobile

Work   Email

Anniversary   Birthday

Notes

Name

Address

Home   Mobile

Work   Email

Anniversary   Birthday

Notes

Name

Address

Home   Mobile

Work   Email

Anniversary   Birthday

Notes

Name

Address

Home   Mobile

Work   Email

Anniversary   Birthday

Notes

Name

Address

Home   Mobile

Work   Email

Anniversary   Birthday

Notes

Name

Address

Home   Mobile

Work   Email

Anniversary   Birthday

Notes

K

Name

Address

Home   Mobile

Work   Email

Anniversary   Birthday

Notes

Name

Address

Home   Mobile

Work   Email

Anniversary   Birthday

Notes

Name

Address

Home   Mobile

Work   Email

Anniversary   Birthday

Notes

L

Name

Address

Home   Mobile

Work   Email

Anniversary   Birthday

Notes

Name

Address

Home   Mobile

Work   Email

Anniversary   Birthday

Notes

Name

Address

Home   Mobile

Work   Email

Anniversary   Birthday

Notes

L

Name

Address

Home   Mobile

Work   Email

Anniversary   Birthday

Notes

Name

Address

Home   Mobile

Work   Email

Anniversary   Birthday

Notes

Name

Address

Home   Mobile

Work   Email

Anniversary   Birthday

Notes

L

Name

Address

Home   Mobile

Work   Email

Anniversary   Birthday

Notes

Name

Address

Home   Mobile

Work   Email

Anniversary   Birthday

Notes

Name

Address

Home   Mobile

Work   Email

Anniversary   Birthday

Notes

L

Name

Address

Home   Mobile

Work   Email

Anniversary   Birthday

Notes

Name

Address

Home   Mobile

Work   Email

Anniversary   Birthday

Notes

Name

Address

Home   Mobile

Work   Email

Anniversary   Birthday

Notes

Name

Address

Home   Mobile

Work   Email

Anniversary   Birthday

Notes

Name

Address

Home   Mobile

Work   Email

Anniversary   Birthday

Notes

Name

Address

Home   Mobile

Work   Email

Anniversary   Birthday

Notes

L

Name

Address

Home   Mobile

Work   Email

Anniversary   Birthday

Notes

Name

Address

Home   Mobile

Work   Email

Anniversary   Birthday

Notes

Name

Address

Home   Mobile

Work   Email

Anniversary   Birthday

Notes

M

Name

Address

Home   Mobile

Work   Email

Anniversary   Birthday

Notes

Name

Address

Home   Mobile

Work   Email

Anniversary   Birthday

Notes

Name

Address

Home   Mobile

Work   Email

Anniversary   Birthday

Notes

M

Name

Address

Home   Mobile

Work   Email

Anniversary   Birthday

Notes

Name

Address

Home   Mobile

Work   Email

Anniversary   Birthday

Notes

Name

Address

Home   Mobile

Work   Email

Anniversary   Birthday

Notes

Name

Address

Home   Mobile

Work   Email

Anniversary   Birthday

Notes

Name

Address

Home   Mobile

Work   Email

Anniversary   Birthday

Notes

Name

Address

Home   Mobile

Work   Email

Anniversary   Birthday

Notes

Name

Address

Home   Mobile

Work   Email

Anniversary   Birthday

Notes

Name

Address

Home   Mobile

Work   Email

Anniversary   Birthday

Notes

Name

Address

Home   Mobile

Work   Email

Anniversary   Birthday

Notes

Name

Address

Home   Mobile

Work   Email

Anniversary   Birthday

Notes

Name

Address

Home   Mobile

Work   Email

Anniversary   Birthday

Notes

Name

Address

Home   Mobile

Work   Email

Anniversary   Birthday

Notes

M

Name

Address

Home   Mobile

Work   Email

Anniversary   Birthday

Notes

Name

Address

Home   Mobile

Work   Email

Anniversary   Birthday

Notes

Name

Address

Home   Mobile

Work   Email

Anniversary   Birthday

Notes

Name

Address

Home   Mobile

Work   Email

Anniversary   Birthday

Notes

Name

Address

Home   Mobile

Work   Email

Anniversary   Birthday

Notes

Name

Address

Home   Mobile

Work   Email

Anniversary   Birthday

Notes

N

Name

Address

Home   Mobile

Work   Email

Anniversary   Birthday

Notes

Name

Address

Home   Mobile

Work   Email

Anniversary   Birthday

Notes

Name

Address

Home   Mobile

Work   Email

Anniversary   Birthday

Notes

Name

Address

Home   Mobile

Work   Email

Anniversary   Birthday

Notes

Name

Address

Home   Mobile

Work   Email

Anniversary   Birthday

Notes

Name

Address

Home   Mobile

Work   Email

Anniversary   Birthday

Notes

N

Name

Address

Home   Mobile

Work   Email

Anniversary   Birthday

Notes

Name

Address

Home   Mobile

Work   Email

Anniversary   Birthday

Notes

Name

Address

Home   Mobile

Work   Email

Anniversary   Birthday

Notes

N

Name

Address

Home | Mobile
Work | Email
Anniversary | Birthday
Notes

Name

Address

Home | Mobile
Work | Email
Anniversary | Birthday
Notes

Name

Address

Home | Mobile
Work | Email
Anniversary | Birthday
Notes

Name

Address

Home   Mobile

Work   Email

Anniversary   Birthday

Notes

Name

Address

Home   Mobile

Work   Email

Anniversary   Birthday

Notes

Name

Address

Home   Mobile

Work   Email

Anniversary   Birthday

Notes

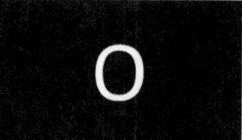

Name

Address

Home   Mobile

Work   Email

Anniversary   Birthday

Notes

Name

Address

Home   Mobile

Work   Email

Anniversary   Birthday

Notes

Name

Address

Home   Mobile

Work   Email

Anniversary   Birthday

Notes

O

Name

Address

Home   Mobile

Work   Email

Anniversary   Birthday

Notes

Name

Address

Home   Mobile

Work   Email

Anniversary   Birthday

Notes

Name

Address

Home   Mobile

Work   Email

Anniversary   Birthday

Notes

Name

Address

Home   Mobile

Work   Email

Anniversary   Birthday

Notes

Name

Address

Home   Mobile

Work   Email

Anniversary   Birthday

Notes

Name

Address

Home   Mobile

Work   Email

Anniversary   Birthday

Notes

O

Name

Address

Home   Mobile

Work   Email

Anniversary   Birthday

Notes

Name

Address

Home   Mobile

Work   Email

Anniversary   Birthday

Notes

Name

Address

Home   Mobile

Work   Email

Anniversary   Birthday

Notes

O

Name

Address

Home   Mobile

Work   Email

Anniversary   Birthday

Notes

Name

Address

Home   Mobile

Work   Email

Anniversary   Birthday

Notes

Name

Address

Home   Mobile

Work   Email

Anniversary   Birthday

Notes

O

Name

Address

Home   Mobile

Work   Email

Anniversary   Birthday

Notes

Name

Address

Home   Mobile

Work   Email

Anniversary   Birthday

Notes

Name

Address

Home   Mobile

Work   Email

Anniversary   Birthday

Notes

P

Name

Address

Home   Mobile

Work   Email

Anniversary   Birthday

Notes

Name

Address

Home   Mobile

Work   Email

Anniversary   Birthday

Notes

Name

Address

Home   Mobile

Work   Email

Anniversary   Birthday

Notes

P

Name

Address

Home   Mobile

Work   Email

Anniversary   Birthday

Notes

Name

Address

Home   Mobile

Work   Email

Anniversary   Birthday

Notes

Name

Address

Home   Mobile

Work   Email

Anniversary   Birthday

Notes

P

Name

Address

Home   Mobile

Work   Email

Anniversary   Birthday

Notes

Name

Address

Home   Mobile

Work   Email

Anniversary   Birthday

Notes

Name

Address

Home   Mobile

Work   Email

Anniversary   Birthday

Notes

P

Name

Address

Home   **Mobile**

Work   **Email**

Anniversary   **Birthday**

Notes

Name

Address

Home   **Mobile**

Work   **Email**

Anniversary   **Birthday**

Notes

Name

Address

Home   **Mobile**

Work   **Email**

Anniversary   **Birthday**

Notes

P

Name

Address

Home   Mobile

Work   Email

Anniversary   Birthday

Notes

Name

Address

Home   Mobile

Work   Email

Anniversary   Birthday

Notes

Name

Address

Home   Mobile

Work   Email

Anniversary   Birthday

Notes

P

Name

Address

Home   Mobile

Work   Email

Anniversary   Birthday

Notes

Name

Address

Home   Mobile

Work   Email

Anniversary   Birthday

Notes

Name

Address

Home   Mobile

Work   Email

Anniversary   Birthday

Notes

Name

Address

Home   Mobile

Work   Email

Anniversary   Birthday

Notes

Name

Address

Home   Mobile

Work   Email

Anniversary   Birthday

Notes

Name

Address

Home   Mobile

Work   Email

Anniversary   Birthday

Notes

Q

Name

Address

Home   Mobile

Work   Email

Anniversary   Birthday

Notes

Name

Address

Home   Mobile

Work   Email

Anniversary   Birthday

Notes

Name

Address

Home   Mobile

Work   Email

Anniversary   Birthday

Notes

Name

Address

Home   Mobile

Work   Email

Anniversary   Birthday

Notes

Name

Address

Home   Mobile

Work   Email

Anniversary   Birthday

Notes

Name

Address

Home   Mobile

Work   Email

Anniversary   Birthday

Notes

Q

Name

Address

Home   Mobile

Work   Email

Anniversary   Birthday

Notes

Name

Address

Home   Mobile

Work   Email

Anniversary   Birthday

Notes

Name

Address

Home   Mobile

Work   Email

Anniversary   Birthday

Notes

Name

Address

Home   Mobile

Work   Email

Anniversary   Birthday

Notes

Name

Address

Home   Mobile

Work   Email

Anniversary   Birthday

Notes

Name

Address

Home   Mobile

Work   Email

Anniversary   Birthday

Notes

Q

Name

Address

Home | Mobile

Work | Email

Anniversary | Birthday

Notes

Name

Address

Home | Mobile

Work | Email

Anniversary | Birthday

Notes

Name

Address

Home | Mobile

Work | Email

Anniversary | Birthday

Notes

R

Name

Address

Home   Mobile

Work   Email

Anniversary   Birthday

Notes

Name

Address

Home   Mobile

Work   Email

Anniversary   Birthday

Notes

Name

Address

Home   Mobile

Work   Email

Anniversary   Birthday

Notes

Name

Address

Home	Mobile
Work	Email
Anniversary	Birthday

Notes

Name

Address

Home	Mobile
Work	Email
Anniversary	Birthday

Notes

Name

Address

Home	Mobile
Work	Email
Anniversary	Birthday

Notes

R

Name

Address

Home   Mobile

Work   Email

Anniversary   Birthday

Notes

Name

Address

Home   Mobile

Work   Email

Anniversary   Birthday

Notes

Name

Address

Home   Mobile

Work   Email

Anniversary   Birthday

Notes

R

Name

Address

Home   Mobile

Work   Email

Anniversary   Birthday

Notes

Name

Address

Home   Mobile

Work   Email

Anniversary   Birthday

Notes

Name

Address

Home   Mobile

Work   Email

Anniversary   Birthday

Notes

R

Name

Address

Home   **Mobile**

Work   **Email**

Anniversary   **Birthday**

Notes

Name

Address

Home   **Mobile**

Work   **Email**

Anniversary   **Birthday**

Notes

Name

Address

Home   **Mobile**

Work   **Email**

Anniversary   **Birthday**

Notes

Name

Address

Home   Mobile

Work   Email

Anniversary   Birthday

Notes

Name

Address

Home   Mobile

Work   Email

Anniversary   Birthday

Notes

Name

Address

Home   Mobile

Work   Email

Anniversary   Birthday

Notes

S

Name

Address

Home   Mobile

Work   Email

Anniversary   Birthday

Notes

Name

Address

Home   Mobile

Work   Email

Anniversary   Birthday

Notes

Name

Address

Home   Mobile

Work   Email

Anniversary   Birthday

Notes

S

Name

Address

Home | Mobile

Work | Email

Anniversary | Birthday

Notes

Name

Address

Home | Mobile

Work | Email

Anniversary | Birthday

Notes

Name

Address

Home | Mobile

Work | Email

Anniversary | Birthday

Notes

S

Name

Address

Home   Mobile

Work   Email

Anniversary   Birthday

Notes

Name

Address

Home   Mobile

Work   Email

Anniversary   Birthday

Notes

Name

Address

Home   Mobile

Work   Email

Anniversary   Birthday

Notes

S

Name

Address

Home   Mobile

Work   Email

Anniversary   Birthday

Notes

Name

Address

Home   Mobile

Work   Email

Anniversary   Birthday

Notes

Name

Address

Home   Mobile

Work   Email

Anniversary   Birthday

Notes

S

Name

Address

Home   **Mobile**

Work   **Email**

Anniversary   **Birthday**

Notes

Name

Address

Home   **Mobile**

Work   **Email**

Anniversary   **Birthday**

Notes

Name

Address

Home   **Mobile**

Work   **Email**

Anniversary   **Birthday**

Notes

S

Name

Address

Home   Mobile

Work   Email

Anniversary   Birthday

Notes

Name

Address

Home   Mobile

Work   Email

Anniversary   Birthday

Notes

Name

Address

Home   Mobile

Work   Email

Anniversary   Birthday

Notes

T

Name

Address

Home   Mobile

Work   Email

Anniversary   Birthday

Notes

Name

Address

Home   Mobile

Work   Email

Anniversary   Birthday

Notes

Name

Address

Home   Mobile

Work   Email

Anniversary   Birthday

Notes

T

Name

Address

Home   **Mobile**

Work   **Email**

Anniversary   **Birthday**

Notes

Name

Address

Home   **Mobile**

Work   **Email**

Anniversary   **Birthday**

Notes

Name

Address

Home   **Mobile**

Work   **Email**

Anniversary   **Birthday**

Notes

T

Name

Address

Home   **Mobile**

Work   **Email**

Anniversary   **Birthday**

Notes

Name

Address

Home   **Mobile**

Work   **Email**

Anniversary   **Birthday**

Notes

Name

Address

Home   **Mobile**

Work   **Email**

Anniversary   **Birthday**

Notes

T

Name

Address

Home   Mobile

Work   Email

Anniversary   Birthday

Notes

Name

Address

Home   Mobile

Work   Email

Anniversary   Birthday

Notes

Name

Address

Home   Mobile

Work   Email

Anniversary   Birthday

Notes

T

Name

Address

Home	Mobile
Work	Email
Anniversary	Birthday

Notes

Name

Address

Home	Mobile
Work	Email
Anniversary	Birthday

Notes

Name

Address

Home	Mobile
Work	Email
Anniversary	Birthday

Notes

T

Name

Address

Home   Mobile

Work   Email

Anniversary   Birthday

Notes

Name

Address

Home   Mobile

Work   Email

Anniversary   Birthday

Notes

Name

Address

Home   Mobile

Work   Email

Anniversary   Birthday

Notes

Name

Address

Home   Mobile

Work   Email

Anniversary   Birthday

Notes

Name

Address

Home   Mobile

Work   Email

Anniversary   Birthday

Notes

Name

Address

Home   Mobile

Work   Email

Anniversary   Birthday

Notes

U

Name

Address

Home   Mobile

Work   Email

Anniversary   Birthday

Notes

Name

Address

Home   Mobile

Work   Email

Anniversary   Birthday

Notes

Name

Address

Home   Mobile

Work   Email

Anniversary   Birthday

Notes

Name

Address

Home   Mobile

Work   Email

Anniversary   Birthday

Notes

Name

Address

Home   Mobile

Work   Email

Anniversary   Birthday

Notes

Name

Address

Home   Mobile

Work   Email

Anniversary   Birthday

Notes

Name

Address

Home   Mobile

Work   Email

Anniversary   Birthday

Notes

Name

Address

Home   Mobile

Work   Email

Anniversary   Birthday

Notes

Name

Address

Home   Mobile

Work   Email

Anniversary   Birthday

Notes

U

Name

Address

Home   Mobile

Work   Email

Anniversary   Birthday

Notes

Name

Address

Home   Mobile

Work   Email

Anniversary   Birthday

Notes

Name

Address

Home   Mobile

Work   Email

Anniversary   Birthday

Notes

U

Name

Address

Home   Mobile

Work   Email

Anniversary   Birthday

Notes

Name

Address

Home   Mobile

Work   Email

Anniversary   Birthday

Notes

Name

Address

Home   Mobile

Work   Email

Anniversary   Birthday

Notes

Name

Address

Home   Mobile

Work   Email

Anniversary   Birthday

Notes

Name

Address

Home   Mobile

Work   Email

Anniversary   Birthday

Notes

Name

Address

Home   Mobile

Work   Email

Anniversary   Birthday

Notes

Name

Address

Home   Mobile

Work   Email

Anniversary   Birthday

Notes

Name

Address

Home   Mobile

Work   Email

Anniversary   Birthday

Notes

Name

Address

Home   Mobile

Work   Email

Anniversary   Birthday

Notes

Name

Address

Home   Mobile

Work   Email

Anniversary   Birthday

Notes

Name

Address

Home   Mobile

Work   Email

Anniversary   Birthday

Notes

Name

Address

Home   Mobile

Work   Email

Anniversary   Birthday

Notes

Name

Address

Home   Mobile

Work   Email

Anniversary   Birthday

Notes

Name

Address

Home   Mobile

Work   Email

Anniversary   Birthday

Notes

Name

Address

Home   Mobile

Work   Email

Anniversary   Birthday

Notes

V

Name

Address

Home   Mobile

Work   Email

Anniversary   Birthday

Notes

Name

Address

Home   Mobile

Work   Email

Anniversary   Birthday

Notes

Name

Address

Home   Mobile

Work   Email

Anniversary   Birthday

Notes

Name

Address

Home   Mobile

Work   Email

Anniversary   Birthday

Notes

Name

Address

Home   Mobile

Work   Email

Anniversary   Birthday

Notes

Name

Address

Home   Mobile

Work   Email

Anniversary   Birthday

Notes

Name

Address

Home   Mobile

Work   Email

Anniversary   Birthday

Notes

Name

Address

Home   Mobile

Work   Email

Anniversary   Birthday

Notes

Name

Address

Home   Mobile

Work   Email

Anniversary   Birthday

Notes

Name

Address

Home   Mobile

Work   Email

Anniversary   Birthday

Notes

Name

Address

Home   Mobile

Work   Email

Anniversary   Birthday

Notes

Name

Address

Home   Mobile

Work   Email

Anniversary   Birthday

Notes

Name

Address

Home   Mobile

Work   Email

Anniversary   Birthday

Notes

Name

Address

Home   Mobile

Work   Email

Anniversary   Birthday

Notes

Name

Address

Home   Mobile

Work   Email

Anniversary   Birthday

Notes

Name

Address

Home   Mobile

Work   Email

Anniversary   Birthday

Notes

Name

Address

Home   Mobile

Work   Email

Anniversary   Birthday

Notes

Name

Address

Home   Mobile

Work   Email

Anniversary   Birthday

Notes

W

Name

Address

Home   Mobile

Work   Email

Anniversary   Birthday

Notes

Name

Address

Home   Mobile

Work   Email

Anniversary   Birthday

Notes

Name

Address

Home   Mobile

Work   Email

Anniversary   Birthday

Notes

W

Name

Address

Home	Mobile
Work	Email
Anniversary	Birthday

Notes

Name

Address

Home	Mobile
Work	Email
Anniversary	Birthday

Notes

Name

Address

Home	Mobile
Work	Email
Anniversary	Birthday

Notes

Name

Address

Home   Mobile

Work   Email

Anniversary   Birthday

Notes

Name

Address

Home   Mobile

Work   Email

Anniversary   Birthday

Notes

Name

Address

Home   Mobile

Work   Email

Anniversary   Birthday

Notes

Name

Address

Home   Mobile

Work   Email

Anniversary   Birthday

Notes

Name

Address

Home   Mobile

Work   Email

Anniversary   Birthday

Notes

Name

Address

Home   Mobile

Work   Email

Anniversary   Birthday

Notes

Name

Address

Home   Mobile

Work   Email

Anniversary   Birthday

Notes

Name

Address

Home   Mobile

Work   Email

Anniversary   Birthday

Notes

Name

Address

Home   Mobile

Work   Email

Anniversary   Birthday

Notes

Name

Address

Home   Mobile

Work   Email

Anniversary   Birthday

Notes

Name

Address

Home   Mobile

Work   Email

Anniversary   Birthday

Notes

Name

Address

Home   Mobile

Work   Email

Anniversary   Birthday

Notes

Name

Address

Home   Mobile

Work   Email

Anniversary   Birthday

Notes

Name

Address

Home   Mobile

Work   Email

Anniversary   Birthday

Notes

Name

Address

Home   Mobile

Work   Email

Anniversary   Birthday

Notes

Name

Address

Home   Mobile

Work   Email

Anniversary   Birthday

Notes

Name

Address

Home   Mobile

Work   Email

Anniversary   Birthday

Notes

Name

Address

Home   Mobile

Work   Email

Anniversary   Birthday

Notes

Name

Address

Home   Mobile

Work   Email

Anniversary   Birthday

Notes

Name

Address

Home   Mobile

Work   Email

Anniversary   Birthday

Notes

Name

Address

Home   Mobile

Work   Email

Anniversary   Birthday

Notes

Name

Address

Home   Mobile

Work   Email

Anniversary   Birthday

Notes

Name

Address

Home   Mobile

Work   Email

Anniversary   Birthday

Notes

Name

Address

Home   Mobile

Work   Email

Anniversary   Birthday

Notes

Y

Name

Address

Home   Mobile

Work   Email

Anniversary   Birthday

Notes

Name

Address

Home   Mobile

Work   Email

Anniversary   Birthday

Notes

Name

Address

Home   Mobile

Work   Email

Anniversary   Birthday

Notes

Name

Address

Home   Mobile

Work   Email

Anniversary   Birthday

Notes

Name

Address

Home   Mobile

Work   Email

Anniversary   Birthday

Notes

Name

Address

Home   Mobile

Work   Email

Anniversary   Birthday

Notes

Name

Address

Home   Mobile

Work   Email

Anniversary   Birthday

Notes

Name

Address

Home   Mobile

Work   Email

Anniversary   Birthday

Notes

Name

Address

Home   Mobile

Work   Email

Anniversary   Birthday

Notes

Name

Address

Home   Mobile

Work   Email

Anniversary   Birthday

Notes

Name

Address

Home   Mobile

Work   Email

Anniversary   Birthday

Notes

Name

Address

Home   Mobile

Work   Email

Anniversary   Birthday

Notes

Z

Name

Address

Home   Mobile

Work   Email

Anniversary   Birthday

Notes

Name

Address

Home   Mobile

Work   Email

Anniversary   Birthday

Notes

Name

Address

Home   Mobile

Work   Email

Anniversary   Birthday

Notes

Z

Name

Address

Home   Mobile

Work   Email

Anniversary   Birthday

Notes

Name

Address

Home   Mobile

Work   Email

Anniversary   Birthday

Notes

Name

Address

Home   Mobile

Work   Email

Anniversary   Birthday

Notes

Z

Name

Address

Home	Mobile
Work	Email
Anniversary	Birthday

Notes

Name

Address

Home	Mobile
Work	Email
Anniversary	Birthday

Notes

Name

Address

Home	Mobile
Work	Email
Anniversary	Birthday

Notes

Z

Name

Address

Home   Mobile

Work   Email

Anniversary   Birthday

Notes

Name

Address

Home   Mobile

Work   Email

Anniversary   Birthday

Notes

Name

Address

Home   Mobile

Work   Email

Anniversary   Birthday

Notes

Z

Name

Address

Home	Mobile
Work	Email
Anniversary	Birthday

Notes

Name

Address

Home	Mobile
Work	Email
Anniversary	Birthday

Notes

Name

Address

Home	Mobile
Work	Email
Anniversary	Birthday

Notes

Z

Name

Address

Home	Mobile
Work	Email
Anniversary	Birthday

Notes

Name

Address

Home	Mobile
Work	Email
Anniversary	Birthday

Notes

Name

Address

Home	Mobile
Work	Email
Anniversary	Birthday

Notes